SALMS

Kuhl House Poets

Mark Levine and Emily Wilson, series editors

SALMS

AARON McCOLLOUGH

POEMS

UNIVERSITY OF IOWA PRESS, IOWA CITY

UNIVERSITY OF IOWA PRESS, IOWA CITY 52242
Copyright © 2024 by Aaron McCollough
uipress.uiowa.edu
Printed in the United States of America

DESIGN BY TERESA W. WINGFIELD

Printed on acid-free paper

LIBRARY OF CONGRESS CATALOGING-IN-PUBLICATION DATA
Names: McCollough, Aaron, author.
Title: Salms / Aaron McCollough.
Description: Iowa City: University of Iowa Press, 2024. | Series: Kuhl House Poets
Identifiers: LCCN 2024008523 (print) | LCCN 2024008524 (ebook) | ISBN 9781609389833 (paperback) | ISBN 9781609389840 (ebook)
Subjects: LCGFT: Poetry.
Classification: LCC PS3613.C37 S25 2024 (print) | LCC PS3613.C37 (ebook) | DDC 811/.6—dc23/eng/20240226
LC record available at https://lccn.loc.gov/2024008523
LC ebook record available at https://lccn.loc.gov/2024008524

to life as it arises, Suzanne

CONTENTS

"For who can look for lesse, that loveth life/strife"

—GEORGE HERBERT

FIRST FORM

We had a tree over us
song opening a sack within it
and all silent but newly charted
territory we would recognize

creatures embarrassed
in a clearing, nested in an illusion
nothing can startle
them

out of. Their entire howl
they swallow as
a darkness now
where no burrow is

Misplacing my own
distance, I prepare
for salutary waters
through the sun beating

The glazier carries an eye
that flares on his back
through the nettles
and gale

The oldest tree shade sure
where it stands,
where it was uprooted

We should or we should not
A moment, two moments
reflected in one turning face

Faint fabric,
faint playing and song
sifted with a stretch of spring light.
Almost a cool sheet

to come back to:
moveable trees at the boundary
and the pliancy
of objects

Hard sleep
with nothing
at its core

This is how we go: a refrain
close to recollected
that sinks from us

We don't hear the song,
we know lung and treetop
and cloud together beside the song
and mouth them to arrive in rhythm

in a room a sea, a bell a sea wave
we become an economical sea
exchanged in air,
always with more sound

We don't know how many chambers
there are but assume we choose
and count each an intimate friend

The rough pine bark gathering
tender pine tree volunteers
to fill the empty hollow up

Preserved in hair, amber,
a tile of earth—
the object's neck
unwinds, we count and walk it down

A study of the morning
or the empty bedroom in a clap of light
turning to look back at night
or never wavering, but

still looking at night
a feeling of movement anyway,
being explained by the mirror

Open and impenetrable clay
orange and blue and carmine
stuck to the earth with the airborne things
the blue blanket of hills

the first leaves, wings banded
in swiveling light
descendant, indehiscent, stranded
twin seeds

Only the breeze, only gravity
only cellulose
only near-sight sky

only time in the fruit
only tree, only trees
and missing the trees

Good morning, shadows
who love us, how we look,
the ripple
around the actual coast of our day

Without knowing our true place,
I pull at my face
Antenna feels the distance
in an open door

Pure tension. Under gravity.
All of what we do is small,
demoralizing.

I organized my day around
nothing, conjuring nothing,
and you actually appeared

The taste is already departing,
only small music
Warm, quiet strangers dance the flowers
"where are my roses? where are my violets?"

Dance the flowers. In the gathering dark,
already a recollection, where ripeness
becomes decay, sensation splits
The dancers mirror the dancers

As they go down, they go up, and
the truth, yeah . . . just a lyre
As the bricks and heat of the day let go

charming almost burning feeling
we would follow into whatever harm
"here are your roses! here are your violets!"

Our animal listening for an
undone drone
to rise between
sound blooms

The low dumb hum
of the down-tuned string
suitable for mourning
song

We have a machine
that imitates this
crushing under a track

It's not a new force in the world
Look how dirty and antiquated
the controls are

My song reaches
the ears of the creatures
whose songs reach me
in this spring dark

It feels familiar:
the songs, the spring, the dark,
so this must be a fold in the path
—those moments are on another side of those hills

Forward is an image:
the reflected music, reflected room,
these close light-forced hems

giving way far off
to the gravel container
left running for your return

A MIRROR

The Wonderful Wood: A Mirror

Wicked men abduct the young. A cruel landlord rides, hunting them who are sent off to safety if they could be. We withdraw from the stream. But not everyone could afford to send their children away.

 Our openness to unfinished distance

One lived with her grandmother who was not well. In a lonely cottage she can't go, nowhere to go and no one to send her. Every space between people and things her hazard. The world we find is not reassuring, certainly. Qualities, bodies, and time. They were too poor, so they hide in the cottage where they earned their bread through piecework and spinning. The only world. They worked with their hands in the cottage near a wonderful wood no one dares go into.

 Light reflected in the open stream

One market day, the old one was too sick to travel. The girl had to go alone to sell their hanks of wool alone. They cried. It was not safe to go, but what choice is there? They had nothing to eat. The world we find. The unfinished one. They cry some more, and bless one another, and then the old one made the girl promise to stick to the public roads and not to take any shortcuts through the too wonderful wood.

 The unfinished wood

And she did go and stick to the public roads with storm clouds of wool on her back. Then, cresting a hill, she caught sight of the cruel landlord riding below her. The girl is calm. The still moment which is the same world. Sunlight just blinks through the overstory, dust hung in it. She walks through the wood, bowing her head to the great oak tree, and she walked through the wood.

A still clearing wood song

The cruel landlord opened his mouth to call out to her kindly, and all he can manage were curses for the great oak, for the girl, for the opening wood. A discontinuous series of states. A history. A different one. His own unfinished wood. The tree addresses the landlord. The great oak called the cruel landlord by his name which is a groan and a summons to the other trees in the wood to close ranks.

Woods in the vast hazard, blinking

The Black Dog: A Mirror

It doesn't matter how much there is to steal, even pennies, robbers would take it. A pair of robbers terrorizing the country-side. The countryside is open. Everyone felt the burden of their crimes; many burdens. In the winter wind, we shivered. The shivering leaves. So, the robbers had their spree, and everyone worried about themselves. Simple sensations are private, they are mine alone.

The old farmer and his wife were not as strong as they had been, and neighbors help when they could. The thing imposes itself. We forget and also did not forget. For the coffin and the cradle and the purse are all against us. The neighbors dragged the old folks out, but they were dead. The thatch fire had not killed them. They had been struck with an iron bar. Shivering, blinking with the whole body. Shivering open.

The alarm is abroad and everyone was looking doubtfully at strangers. The image he sees in the mirror was not him. The ~~robbers~~ murderers kept moving, hiding in the daylight and kept in the shadows at night, on their way out of the county. That is to say, menaced. They were headed for the county line and the great boundary forest that could give them some cover.

In their bloodiness, they have forgotten something about this route. Hunted by a posse, scared, thinking only of escape and rest, they forget that no one ever took this way to the forest after dark—especially with a bad conscience. Animal world. Energy world. Rock world. In the presence of the mirror, he is confused and turns away to the objects that for him were fundamental.

But they enter the forest and remember. The Black Dog of the western woods, who could smell the guilt on death's garments, whose master is death. The image he sees in the mirror is a kind of compliment, and his master's caress recalls him to his body.

The Hill Hound: A Mirror

About sunset, a short and lucky time, a boy, a carpenter's helper,
sees something while heading home. A wounded dog. Our old
companion. He sees white and red fur. He saw in the bushes
coming home at dusk a foot-sore foxhound. He thought so and
got on his haunches and calls to it kindly, "Come back to the
kennels slow and careful." The streetlight blinks out, traced in the
air like a cooling ember. Our old companion. "And I'll wrap your
poor feet in wet leaves to cool them." He calls to it with an offer
of help. Down to only a hint of light, another habit, another ghost.

No response. He prepares a bandage, dandelion leaves dipped
in the nearby stream. Called the dog again. A little light can be
warm, even just the memory of it. A short lucky time. A surprise
comes out of the bush, white coat and big cloudy ears, larger than
a calf and rough. Eyes of muggy fire and racing clouds. It was
one of the fairy dogs who token death. Asking after meaning.
Is it there or only an idea?

Asking-after-meaning-sickness. The places in which I find myself.

The boy regains his composure. He knew you must become
invisible, motionless, silent, and try to smell like a dead thing,
yet he reaches out for the great pads one by one. He bandages

them. "Go away to your home. I go home to mine." Objects are never foreign to the senses. Another myself in the same world. Another sunset.

Another sunset on the same dark road the same boy met a wild goat, cave-matted cashmere and horns. Bright yellow eyes and the cloud it leaves in one's own vision. He couldn't run, where can he run? The shrieking goat was on him hoofs and horns. The same world in which we find ourselves.

And then, from the same air on to the goat's back our old companion. The two unket things tore each other until the woods ring by the light from their eyes their too physical weight.

The goat gets the worst of it and changed. The goat is an owl. It flies away. If there was a hound, it is hidden and barely the dank smell of its coat. May we not be satisfied, nor even be healed, perhaps we may be consoled.

The Wounded Swan: A Mirror

On one marsh, the wild birds left the water to the swans. You step out of it like a garment. There were hundreds nobody bothered. They were afraid to shoot at them or steal their eggs. There were hundreds, there were seven. Seven swans terrify the surrounding folks. It's the same world. Animals might, or what that might indicate.

If you hear the armor clatter of their flying over, run home and bar your doors against the world. The people who lived by hunting birds did so and went hungry. An old rag that was rancid-smelling as if it were an animal. One boy couldn't shiver, he is always unafraid. There was a young fowler who was hungry. Everyone was, and they could not eat their effort, but no one dared to touch a swan.

The sweat of the brow, the discharge of abscesses, cobwebs, dead cockroaches, alum, and sand. When he bowed to pick up the wounded bird, the other six laid into him. His boat drifted aground or he would have drowned. He stepped out of it like a garment, took the swan home, and bound up its injured wing. The slime to the wounded bark.

How could he kill it? The mysterious blood blemishes everything it touched. And what could he do when the swan changes into a blue-lipped girl, except take her for his wife? The image he sees in the mirror is the same world. And he was not surprised when, every night, the six swans flew around his hut and beat on the door. He laughs the way frightened people laugh: water echoing somewhere in the cave.

Coral bones buoyed in the drift. As he sees himself, one not allowed to be rescued, I saw him, solid ground beneath the weight of me. He kept his new wife for seven days, and then her wounded arm was healed and feathered. She was becoming a swan again, and she is a swan, hissing and battering him with her tremendous arm-wings. As if it were an animal. He runs from her sweeping wings, and the seven swans lay into him. They held him down in the deepest part of the marsh, and then they fly away. No wild birds go there. It was always empty.

Imagination: A Mirror

An innkeeper's sons, bored after their daily chores, begin to play at the problems of older people. The first announces himself a cutpurse, grabbing his brother's tobacco, and ran into the thicket adjoining the inn. The aggrieved names himself the magistrate, his little brothers deputies, and the middle brother hangman. This reversal takes place before our eyes.

Justice must be served, and the little ones are deputed into the dense bushes to locate the fugitive. The second brother sits in his chair calmly overseeing the hangman's work, and the big mulberry was shortly a makeshift gallows. The other side of things must already be visible in the environment in which we live. From the cries of the deputies and the tauntings of the thief, we know everyone is enjoying the game, and their voices soon became louder, more excited as the hunt concludes.

So, the first brother was found, and the second brother announces the decree. Thinking nothing of a distant shot deep in the thicket, the little ones deliver their brother up to the hangman who, not knowing any better, slips a noose over the brother's head and pulled it tight only for a moment to hang him. Just sipping at the authority of death.

Only, the sudden disorder—a feral pig, grunting and squealing and snuffling, crashes into the clearing, trampled one of the deputies, shrieking now in pain and terror, scattered the brothers—interrupts the game, which is now not that. The relation of the image to the model is disturbed and confused. The wounded pig with its blood left all around the clearing and on the high grass at the edge, they thought was the devil come to punish them for playing such a nasty game. But there was no devil, only the pig, and themselves, and the problems of older people.

A Peasant: A Mirror

A rich man's son, raised as he was in opulence and without opportunity to go hungry, is often bored. Exhausting, having exhausted the danger and excitements of hunting in the hills, he began going to the village and looking for a girl. I always stumble on some particular perception or other. As he goes, he is finding boys often more available to his intention, a development he accepts and comes to embrace. There were many boys in the village, many of them desperate for a few crowns. At least someone is stumbling.

Once, in the throes of an embrace, the rich man's son was stunned to gaze upon his own face reflected in his night's companion. He doubts himself, but gripping the other boy firm he grew certain, they have the same face. He stumbles away in fear, and for months he stopped his carousing. Keeping one's promise does indeed appear to stand as a challenge to time. But soon, he is exhausted again with the monotony of his own lack of need. Fullness itself can make him hungry. And again, he was with the boys of the village, so much so, he begins to recognize them, to know them. A denial of change, even if my desire were to change.

With the weeks and months, the rich man's son found himself happier in the village than he is at home. He sleeps in his own bed rarely. One morning, he is forced to return, having exhausted credit and coin. One evening, returning home from the village, he happened to catch through an open dormer his father and himself speaking cordially. The explanation is obvious, it must be the boy from the village, the double, assuming my role, enjoying my comforts while I slept rough. Character has a history, which it has "contracted," one might say. One evening, he found he has been replaced and is enraged.

The easy life he scorns now appears enchanting. He is growing nostalgic. He can think of nothing but how to reclaim his place. Bloody with jealousy, consumed by thoughts of his lost entitlements, the rich man's son lay in wait in the hills where he has, long before, tired of hunting. Soon, just as he expects, a small hunting party arrives, his enemy among them.

The rich man's son manages to surprise his enemy alone in a hollow. The two embrace again with a different conclusion. The pretender is slain. But his face, which lately had been identical to the rich man's son, looks different in death. We say that x and y are wearing the same suit—that is, clothes that are so similar they are interchangeable with no noticeable difference. What had happened, how has he killed this man, another rich man's son? He does not stick around to find out. He fled to the village and then on to a further village, where he will not be recognized, where no one would have sought him, where new habits must be enough to sustain him. And he remains the prince whom he remembers having been, and he becomes the peasant whom other people continued to observe.

Either / Or: A Mirror

There they were. There was a girl who often sees things that were not there. A boy often failed to see what was. What was there wasn't—just for him, something resting, something that remained in agitated repose. Everyone else knows it is there. In crossing the room, they swerve to avoid tripping on it, and he does, but ask him why and he would tell you a fable about a clearing in the unfinished wood. How illogical the movements in logic must be, since the negative is evil.

She, sometimes seeing a devil in the pottery, a rustic fiend in the sink drain, would cry out "wait!" so that everybody, startled, holds off. Whatever we are doing, we looked to her. The boy would look for an explanation. Wait for what? What wasn't there that was—just for her, something restless, constantly reproducing itself or being repressed. Crows feet stark around the curtains. A real or an ideal possibility.

Veritable, though offensive to the understanding. An innocent vision of the sun or its eclipse. There is a boy, and there is a girl, and I am always surprised to hear music here of all places. Its manner of coming into the world presupposed by the fact that it is.

A Mystery Play

The first sir self said "I cannot speak." The second sir same
"I learned it from you." "To speak?" self. "The same," same. The
self-same first, saying "I knew I'm always before you," could not
speak for himself. In the middle of the air stood he. Far below lies
sir same, a jumble of wet chips, his head still singing as it rolls.

[sings] "I recognize you of old. Thinking of time in that subtle way."

"You've never known me," sir self refrains from saying. "Only
what you say yourself," refraining still.

[sings] "dry old bone, spot of paint, pot of pain"

"If you say so"

[no longer singing] "I do not say, I sing, old saint, who took my
ardor for a wine butt"

"You'd drown in it and the ignominy of boyhood."

"It threatens without destroying. You could say it resembles me,"
sir same, admiring the reflection he is buoyed on.

"I couldn't say, but would recall you to a promise."

"What promise, listener, except to be recalled, I know it, and to love
the recollection, cursed blessed homesick, sour, instigating song."

salm 10.22

Having been told we were moving to a mountain, I saw a
triangle with a house tumbling down its edge.

A little girl named Ruth died of leukemia—I lay in my bed and
thought about a lovely portrait weeping in distant dark.

My legs began to ache around then, and my thighs turned the
color of an eggplant.

My astronomy of death then imagined a distant God whose
planet could never be reached but whom I respected as an
element: oxygen and the floor.

On the cooking basket weave of my mother's volkswagen,
sex was described.

I sat in my own shit as the faucet violently filled the bath,
parents looming between anger and fear, asking is there
anything wrong? do you need to tell us something?

Language being a peccant inheritance none of us suspected, we
all kept speaking, filling the air. What seemed like days passed.

salm 12.13 *resurrection, imperfect.*

Visiting a friend of my mother's in Atlanta, it was a boy I never
met again who showed me an illustration from one of his
father's books depicting rear entry, saying that's what your
parents do, leaving me dismayed and lonely in my universe.

And then Bucky and I saw two dogs in a bend in the road,
and I thought so that's it, and was calm.

And again later, what seemed like years but could have been
weeks, with Andrew and Felix at their father's apartment,
I saw it in a film and hated it and hated my father.

Did all that seed me?

An older boy told me a vagina felt like grape jelly before he
convinced me to take off all my clothes for him. It was years,
I imagined women filled with grape jelly.

Already born and reborn, snake-piled with assertions about my
making and what I was made to do. *Sleep sleep old Sun thou canst
not have repast / As yet /* (Donne).

salm 12.13

Riding in the car I used to focus my eyes on the bucket seat
and let my vision blur as the sounds of my parents' voices sank
beneath the engine gnarl. My body did not disappear, but I left
them and the little capsule carved by their talk and touch.

During the slow, carving climb up the mountain, my father once
turned to me and said *I always felt I was an angel of war.*

I stood in the pea gravel drive, next to the utility pole with the
transformer I worried about, and stared at a constellation of
stones, thinking *I will grow and change and leave, this gravel will
wash away, but I can remember this picture forever.*

Because the soul is there, behind the face, *which comprehendeth
all unbounded space* (Traherne).

salm 2.12 *clouds didymus, judas the twin*

Innocence—whatever we mean by the term—does not just
go away in a shock, as the phrase "loss of innocence" suggests—
or, "the Fall." If we lose it, we do so entropically: the cooling
of a humid condition (physical life) that leads to snowfall

    have you found the beginning then, he said

Thought not   All the now long-growing day
still knots, still clouds diaphragm between abdomen
and chest: my own life, urine, sweat, saliva like
tears—interstitials falling from the mixture, frost in eden

    , that you look to the end (the Gospel of Thomas)

I do remember condensation and the mildew smell of most
of the world's rooms before I really had to speak for myself
found feelings determined ideas
find ideas in feelings you feel you know the word for

you may cloud and break the cloud
that feeling forming in your chest

nothing is conserved, something just begins

those shadows of clouds in summer
slowly darkening the asphalt before
the rain darkens it more

salm 2.23 didymus passion

I split wood for proof the wound is real, just
to make sure the kingdom of god is within

My concern is like sunlight focused on an anthill
sufficient unto the day's confusion

that which befalleth . . . beasts (Ecclesiastes)
and this morning a sinkful of dishes is swarming with pismires

my concern is like
myself bent over their furious movements,

pinched down and hived into an insect of attention,
a real present, though this is the memory

salm 05.24

I was especially alone. I would go to the far edges of whatever grounds were allowed and then crawl through the branches of the unkempt bushes there. In that cool dark, I would watch to see cars beyond the fence, passing toward what I imagined were even darker, cooler removes. Honeysuckle and clean sandy dirt breeze morphine.

Often the need to evacuate rose up strongly almost like temptation or lust. Sitting there, moving as little as possible, savoring it. What was it, not a hunger, the opposite of that, or its obverse: not to be thrown into the world.

Another secret, I guess. But one that obviously couldn't be kept. My own putrefaction. I remember the panic in my parents' voices, with the bathwater rushing: "Is anything wrong?" And I remember answering truthfully, "No, nothing's wrong."

salm 11.8

I'm real. The weight of me impresses the long grass of the lawn
of the only people I know.

My soul sits at a walnut table. The harsh rhythm of minor
blasphemy tickles my skin but means only "beware the
inexorable treachery of the world's appearances."

The Lord may need rest, but we are in a wild place of rivers.

I'm very real, with a stairwell long and dark in my own eye and
the fruit I bear an inconvenient season. Acorns crash on the
deck outside. A feeling like want.

We want protection.

Day and night do not pass, they adhere, and roll together under
uneven weight, a good measure, pressed down, shaken, and
running over,

a grateful kind of losing.

salm 12.15 *sigh & grone*

Before almost anything else happened, I knew we were naked
in the garden. Before that only a bike without handle grips,
a plastic-potted cactus, people standing in ritual sadness.
We were naked, only us and the objects: a tent draped over a
swing set, a sandbox and its toys. The temple within the tomb.

Oh, do not mistake a scattering of leaves for a snake, or if it
is a snake suffer it dozing in the domino of shade and sun;
its sting turns red and brown in time before falling to be
covered in snow.

Your fabrics, your face of the waters, only a thought that may
have been had, déjà vu between two mountains. A tent draped
over a swing set, these grounds so necessary to tomb and
temple, nakedness the fire of being precisely here for this
cornstalk calm calamity near the others.

Now the wind chime recalls me to a cooling afternoon, duly
clothed. One might even say, bundled.

salm 02.03

The gorge in the mountain
is the beginning of disappearance,
but that's how the sun
works its way from the air
to the center of the earth

(like rain upon the fleece,
and as showers falling gently [Psalm 72])

and the sun carries the creatures,
or they find themselves there

My father says most fish die
from the fright,
even after they're released,

but before that it feels fine
to throw a baited hook
out in their way,
and when one takes it,
the tensed line through the border
of nature opens a frame
as large in your body
as all the flooded caves
beyond the dam,
lighted with water and slivered
with hyalescent forms

salm 12.24

What is a hard heart? A heart is a little room inside a little room, etc., one of infinite stanzas stacked between water and sky.

> *We are close prisoners all . . .*
> *though within larger walls* (Donne).

Usually made of waste fabric, the heart's room is white. The veil of earth should always be clouded with blushing scars from the ground's congestion, but empty, downed capillaries echo the sounds of an old spring trickling in a cave.

And we paint the walls another tenant painted in a sturdy understanding with the elements.

What if these feelings of unreality were the evidence one sought, love's scattered work working itself out in spasm and sense?: yesterday, it was Christmas, tomorrow is Christmas Eve. I feel sad to pass into these less-long nights because my heart is less open. The air smells of eggs in the valley and in the hills.

salm 11.29 *the gospel of judas*

Concluding that wisdom is in contradiction compassed, did he
finally do his betrayal and receive a luminous visitation, mere
fragments of which find their way to us: "generation of" "trees
without fruit" "cloud incorruptible and spirit loan" [—about five
lines missing—].

After that Jesus laughed, not at them but the error of the stars.

> *a grave*
> *too big for me* (Herbert)
> *melancholy tuned heavenly*

With Suzanne, the moral difference between theft and more
violent crimes or alone the sins of omission/commission. I said
some things rise above context, then doubted which was which
when I wash only the plate I ate from.

The face of the soul—my face, rather, but not the visible one—
like a mirror itself, reflects (and therefore comprehends) every-
thing, *The bones, the joints, and that which else remains / Within
that curious fabric* (Traherne).

As Adam again and again, from the spine of the great ridge
o'erlooking history, weeping before sleep.

Down there through the blue-tinged distance and smoke rise
shiny green clottings of privacy and common ground: white oak,
sassafras, tulip tree, sugarberry, elm.

THE SURVIVAL
OF IMAGES

"The past grows without ceasing"

Set off by anything
One hill set so against another

Memory can be an echo that just gets louder

A spring morning like this one,
inside this face
beneath the gentle gnaw of light

Those other faces and hectic worlds
we skipped across the lake

Were you speaking and were
the sun and green grass shining
in your hair

I was filled
with belief
walking down my hill alone

[The sudden wreckage leaves no choice;]

The sudden wreckage leaves no choice;
Slow accumulation also chokes you.
I keep clearing my throat.
Will nothing but poems be enough
to dress us for the occasion
Or will something unexpected emerge,
the hidden urge for song's opposite,
that this was what we wanted all along:
they miss me.
But when the end came, there was none,
no mourning, no end,
just words, dammed up,
words undammed
or lying here and there
like the dusty stars.

Unconditional

There is the sea
How vastly it needs living up to

Forget your container of soil

The fields flare over in conference
    a hoed stone sings

That you were one whose survival
only goes into shore

the tongue the tide
while the deep fields

curl below a close limit

preamble from the heart

In everything withheld
belongs the outward world
as it does with indifference
and the genie obeys the ones
whose treasures
dose them

It is the spirit
here rains
or shines
on a thread

And only one who descends
to the loved one,
    only the knife,
gets bread

preamble from the heart

Not cowardly, not afraid to let
the secret being stolen
steal in upon
the love hidden in thought

to let it
secret, love, and thought
twine in coils
and cinch up every ligament

more tightly with each untimely
turn—
never able to wrench
out of it

Until, even as
the seized sums,
wrenched
at every nerve,

pinprick solemn silence

Not at Bemerton

The halo of suffering protested
our skinny outstretched limbs
collected at base, same lid
seen from beginning to end,
which goes largely hidden
by the orientation of the sun:
his head leant over the banister
folded around itself like an eel

The protest against real suffering
so great
it beggars belief,
redounds with the tide to its halo,
a verge of wet sand

Suffering suffering so small
barely noticed syllable
suffered, protested piously

The criticism of the protest
against suffering which is
the halo of living here
which is real suffering

Totentanz, Sevendies

The kid who smelled of mildew
now remembered takes no offense
he's earth and copulates with shells

shells held to his song
as a gray moth like ash on the wind
mothwise lands and turns into ash

In this rustic nowhere, we find our setting
a wasp hunched on the wing
what is, giving thanks for what is

The stars are a mobile after all
The stars are a jellyfish out on the sand,
sand which is also stars

Lord Cloud

Thanks to the thin wind the ancestors sleep sweetly.
In light rain, our pain still mysterious,
we sip more coffee and "that which arises."

Flaked colors cling to the car window.
For the idea of the sentimental dead,
we repeat ourselves, decal on top of decal.

And we need this quilt of birdsong
with a few shadows in the yard,
a manifest coolness down the little gorge,

the unheard lines that lie here
and rain from our drift into sleep.
Else, where should we seek our pale delight.

And become something else
more accustomed to gravity, all heavy cheer.

Cloud's Fallacies

Cloud prints on transparencies of sky
Some of these, the closer ones, are pulled in and out of view
Today the forecast of rain is being ignored by blue
Who can tell it what is coming, how gentle green
must be struck, slicked, and stuck to itself and the ground
when it stands so far away, almost nowhere as I understand things
I cannot tell it, I am only listening
to the forecast, the galvanic bird lines kicking into each other,
what cannot be wrong about what lies ahead
and these winds know coming up from the valley
and over the ridge so the trees in between know too,
flicked into a stir by knowing because they're green
How can we, being too inhabited,
say anything to what seems
our too far away, imaginary friend

Not Here

Is a wreath of great returns silted into pointed arches
and rib vaults, where, as we walk, we note
how authentic a hand-lettered sign,
where "air-conditioned" cracks and fades
from the glass, as if it knows
it is a voice trailing off with its first audience.

The sweat of old summer dried fast sharp
at the threshold, and the day's long blur
straightened out into a cool moment,
it once said, where expectation could begin
a progress toward utility.

Reading Herbert (2003)

The premonition of the hour of the end
comes this close to us: the floor.
Several moments sweeping in a corner—
the doors all open—sweeping up wind.

The proper response to the time being sadness,

into the face we hope into
$$\text{desires}$$

pending chandelier we would grasp—
confounding, gilded distance caught in the eye's

$$\text{not-light.}$$

To comprehend our own building,

we crumble, God. But that is not like us.

Wind

In a place famous for great wind
it turns on.

The wind chime wildly improvises
its loops of strange time.

Birds in this wish
unperturbed as the wind,
their element,
breaks over their hollow bones
like thought, are

at its height, maybe,
a little quiet, waiting
to see how things are going to go

forever. How that will be.

Until the fervor passes, and what's left
is everyday still.

[The birds are chirping Chopin in the void]

The birds are chirping Chopin in the void

Where the subject at hand is trust,
Abraham is holding Isaac against a rock

The missing tree in the stump
groans at no wind
so deep in rot and
bound for a hole

The missing song in the missing tree
of no sparrow, not the sostenuto prelude

The system is complete
no sparrow falls

Of a Land, a River and Hills

I.

The one who turns his ear has turned his feet.
He turns his head to turn his ear to better hear
the sound and hearing it better, has lifted his feet
to approach the sound he has heard.

What he heard and follows, his fog,
was he knew no song.
Everyone knows. The unfilled note
does what everyone fears: grows.

2.

Or, as he approaches, it seems to grow.
As he turned, it might have slowed
its growth, but now the sound unfolds,
unbends a bed aflow

from firmness, pried out
from settled sky, the cleaved tone,
not song, he cleaves to soot
just outside himself. On his skin.

3.

There it was and completely gone.
Not in bird clatter nor highway tides,
in secret from him, by an underground sea
carved off in other sunken noise,

and, having so turned, his feet
forgot his ear. His ear was lost.
Disowned.
All was folded under the drum of hills.

4.
This body. You turn to feel what you can reach.
The undone, stranger now, wanders
that landscape menaced by ghosts,
the exhaustion of expecting more;

more ghosts, more signal sound,
more stitched interval
inside-out chord: the land, river, hills
meeting each other underfoot.

5.
The river, always filthy, smells burnt,
and the blue hills trail rotten debris.
Still, they are more.
The sound of your step

returning to the sound, a way to resume,
the hills repeating the river's course
reflected by your own distance,
unfinished at the bright brim of a word.

MERE _____

Gateway

In the gateway to the west,
a police bomb truck blocks
the entrance to the Masonic temple,
"In the hollow of the cornerstone,"
I hear one of them say
and think this a fine way to go

Death has overwritten everything
in your song, I say again
as way of observing
you are not dead to me,

as you might say,
but persist inside that word "you,"
which is outside everyone
and also inside them and

as you might also say,
the you I mean
when I address myself

After all this effortful being,
just those letters that open and close
the little vault we build on

One Gather

I came here for some company in my sin,
knowing from loneliness how company can
unstick my genius for it—hence no drinking alone
—and no one minds my song is stolen
It's the way with sin, with song,
there is no one righteous, no, not one,
to bring others along, to look for encouragement
in the same sewer a friend went.
Not for doing wrong.
For taking comfort.

Transparency

Being seen to show the world one's insides,
to let the sun frankly describe
only the hard things it cannot pass through,
not the window. The window
is transparent. Is said to be
transparent, it's see-through,
a sentence made from clear words,
precisely uttered, accurately heard.

The sentence of death is like a window.
It opens on a drawing of a window.

When I kept silence, my bones roared,
says the psalmist, whose heart also melts
like wax in a more hidden place.

Cracked Instrument

I.
thinking what a crack is
far from anything like a sea

addition subtraction
so rigid
a fold gives up

prodigious black wasps noose
and knot themselves by
the streetlight
balistraria

climbers, chargers, dismemberers
unwind an echo in air on
matted leaf and stone

calm permission at the crosswalk:
there is no danger
now you may cross

2.
twig across vista

pressing a natural tower beneath which
deposited leaves wilt in the stream

the rumored pinch of
silty bottom fish slipt between nails

an opening and wider,
the valley and the sky spread
against each other against
us:

the beetle wing veins
in the urinal

3.
smell of dish soap
and tupperware
on cool hands on that hot little face

this air a reservoir
for preserving
spent meaning still suited
to the remaining time

answers
as traffic

with a butterfly not fluttering
its hands in prayer

"Knowledge . . . as reflected in a mirror"

One magnolia blossom on a low branch,
one swift cloud caught
above the little inlet mudflat (ghost)
in grapevine creeper and honeysuckle—
Being lyrical as always, how else
can we be in the afternoon
listening to the neighbor's beliefs
against the world's assertion
that it
is real
                  That voice,
we say, is not the same as what we have
but how shall we compare,
who are bound to respond
but dazed since birth

transformed by degrees
into a stag, the linden embracing the oak

Mere: Of Lakes and Pills

The fretful song I sing
myself drumming my own trunk
the site of the old fort, a few stones
arranged where the walls were

My mouthful of teeth
sinking in the moss
I sense, infected by the public lake
and gassy cave system the soul sills

a mild breeze sneaked
scent of what are those white flowers
and diesel smoke hamburger and fries,
familiar as tuesday

The singer, the dancer, the caster of birth charts
steps out skinned in bark coat
changed by too much
hierophantic congress

Faith in business hours,
the soothing downward pressure
containers place on the scale
once helped me sleep

Mere: Of the Made Wood

The fretful song I sing
midroad of the wild
an "installation" circled with iron palings

The ordinary stone
describes the form of the wave
that delivered it. The hoof clatter,

the restive tidal traffic
of wildfire, the huntsman
humming dry needles,

the siren's elastic lash
on calm water

In the forest, noises of construction
and violation lead to this clearing

—a recording, performed for us
as though we were trees

Mere: Of the Milderness

The fretful song I sing
to take my rifle apart, clean each piece,
then throw it all in the little waves of the lake

to soak my stinging fingers,
cut with fiberglass
splinters in the cloud of my lungs

where love's prayer's footing is
next to the cabinet in my heart,
internal finality, all the elements

conspiring for the greatest good
and also an external one:
merely a sprouting bud

on knotted limbs, the song's interval

Not at Duino

What to do with the choice left by
what one would never choose,
having already acquiesced
to the routine of preceding days
as instruction for rest.
Become the sound of a door closing
against the quiet morning
and gravel's crisp responses to departure,
the modest music slowed and stretched
on a pleasant unseasonable chill.

The hero's way is not here,
but the day remains. It stands
Like a hero's day—must be climbed.
And the choice waits also.
The feelings that pass
like putting on a vest, stand.

The trees, the entire ardent inhuman life
with the gray-washed sky stands
for the music of what to do.

Dove

Morning. I can't see the sun, but
the light in the sky grows
like all things, only as I look away.

The branches amiably nod in breeze
The drowsy smelling magnolia blossoms
now stand in burst white luxury.

Out of the usual commotion, some birds
drop or glide across my view,
but most call from obscurity.

Behind the others, in front of them,
a dove in five beats, the second
so forceful it breaks apart but

still carries. Is that the mournful part,
the high shredded echo,
unmistakable but impossible to locate,

or is it the slowness of the song,
and that pause, where prayers go,
while it thinks about who is gone?

Fossils, Literally, Obtained by Digging

Sitting at a second-story window
atop a steep hill

We stand on ground,
and the ground,
despite its murk,
reflects us; Vermeer,
in painting a mirror,
used colors we shouldn't expect, thus
what the ground is may ask
what it stands on
(and what that reflects)

Fossils, literally, obtained by digging,
preserve the chitinous facts
Our words are thoughts
of water, fire, dust
about wind-touched wing
wasp on rancid pear

I must stop seeing and
remember I was
now in another room
I call remembering something

Magnolia green, holly berry green
spines of the yellow green brush
wrinkled hill entrusted with reflection
A stream against which I cannot go

ACKNOWLEDGMENTS

DURING THE NINE YEARS of writing that led to this book, a handful of readers encouraged and sustained my work. In particular, Martin Corless-Smith's friendship and interest were a real gift. Without our dialogue over this period, the book wouldn't exist. Peter Streckfus, Sally Keith, Karla Kelsey, and James Shea also generously spent time with various versions of this manuscript as I made my way through its wilderness. Finally, thank you, Mark Levine, whose enduring interest and whose teaching have been foundational to the entire strange project of my mature writing life.

Some of the poems in this collection have been previously published in the following publications: *Annulet* ("The Wonderful Wood: A Mirror," "The Black Dog: A Mirror," "The Wounded Swan: A Mirror"); *Interim* ("*Salm* 11.8," "*Salm* 2.12 *clouds didymus, judas the twin*," "*Salm* 12.24"); *The Tiny* ("Cracked Instrument"); *West Branch* ("[Open and impenetrable clay]," "[Good morning, shadows]," "Not at Bemerton").

KUHL HOUSE POETS